Strange Angels

Other Works by William Pitt Root

Sublime Blue: Selected Early Odes of Pablo Neruda

White Boots: New and Selected Poems of the West

The Storm and Other Poems

Trace Elements from a Recurring Kingdom

Faultdancing

The Unbroken Diamond: Night Letter to the Mujahideen

Reasons for Going It on Foot

Invisible Guests

A Journey South

In the World's Common Grasses

Fireclock

Coot and Other Characters

The Port of Galveston

Striking the Dark Air for Music

Strange Angels

New Poems

William Pitt Root

WingsPress
San Antonio, Texas
2013

Strange Angels © 2013 by William Pitt Root

Cover image: "Stalker" © 2013 by Al Kogel.
Interior images from the "Brain Teasers" series © 2013 by Al Kogel.
Used by permission of the artist.

First Edition

Print Edition ISBN: 978-1-60940-319-5

Ebooks:
ePub ISBN: 978-1-60940-320-1
Kindle ISBN: 978-1-60940-321-8
Library PDF ISBN: 978-1-60940-322-5

Wings Press
627 E. Guenther
San Antonio, Texas 78210
On-line catalogue and ordering:
www.wingspress.com
All Wings Press titles are distributed to the trade by
Independent Publishers Group • www.ipgbook.com

Library of Congress Cataloging-in-Publication Data:

Root, William Pitt, 1941-
  [Poems. Selections]
  Strange Angels : new poems / William Pitt Root. -- First Edition.
    pages cm
  Includes index.
  ISBN 978-1-60940-319-5 (pbk. : alk. paper) -- ISBN 978-1-60940-320-1 (ebook)
  -- ISBN 978-1-60940-321-8) -- ISBN 978-1-60940-322-5
  I. Title.
  PS3568.O66A6 2013
  811'.54--dc23
                          2013023524

Contents

Neither Basalt Ledge nor Turnip, or: Forests and Fields

A Flower of Human Light

Fools, Soothsayers and Kings

This book is for Pam who has generously shared over
three decades of her life with me
& to Jennifer Lorca, my daughter, whose presence always
makes my heart applaud with delight

& to Happy my wolfish white companion who tries
to help me become a better wolf
& to Zazu who keeps Happy young
& to SadieKat who has wisely established herself as leader of the pack,
& to my Swedish angel-bro Stewe Claeson with whom
I became best friends at first sight
& to my angel-bro Maj Ragain whose poetry employs
the world's tenderest knockout punch
& to Peter Warshall, recently arrived in Paradise,
even now improving on infrastructures there
while being brought up to date by all those he knows
who've arrived before him
& to Tim "without whom," who leaves behind for each and every one
of his much-loved daughters the puzzle of such
raucous, tender memories as our lives are made of
& to Albert "no angels here" Kogel for his friendship
and fabulous work among these pages

& this book is for all who've never had a book dedicated to them before
& for my all of my beloveds be they living flesh, or ashes, or as yet unborn,
& for some of my enemies (in the hope they may yet become friends)
& especially for anyone who might feel left out
or who still pays for books in hard cash.

Strange Angels

God gives to everything alike,
and as flowing forth from God things are all equal;
angels, men, and the creatures proceed from God
alike in their first emanation....
Any flea as it is in God is nobler than the highest of the angels in himself.

—Meister Eckhart

For man is an amphibian. He lives half in given reality, half in the
home-made universe of symbols. We are like icebergs, immersed in
language but projecting into immediate experience.

—Aldous Huxley

What is the knocking?
What is the knocking at the door in the night?
It is somebody wants to do us harm.
No, no, it is the three strange angels.
Admit them, admit them.

—D.H. Lawrence

Every angel is terrible.

—R.M. Rilke

I don't believe in angels myself but apparently
they believe in me—they keep popping up.

—Maxx Aardman

Night Poem in the Shawangunks

Last night, late,
scribbling letters
behind our house
in the lean-to porch,

I heard abrupt thrashing
from the bottomland
then cries over and over
from some creature

now bird-like, wings beating,
now cat-like, caterwauling.
I couldn't hear the grinding
down of bones and skull

or suckle of the heart
likely seized, still beating,
from a breast among wet weeds,
and yes my own heart quickly

sympathized, first contracting
fearful as the prey's,
then expanding
wanton as a pulsing star,

gaudy as an Aztec priest.
I turned off the light awhile.
I kept my eyes level
with the moonless woods.

Why I Remember

Illustration by Albert Kogel.

Seagrape Tree and the Miraculous

1.

The laboratories explain it away in retrospect as chemistry,
a compound in the pitch; their researchers
have worked with it for years, experimenting
on cataracts in caged rats and drugged monkeys.

Alfredo Verona, at 92, in Miami's Little Havana,
a free man too poor for doctors, never had heard of
such researchers the day he reached out
to the seagrape tree, the night he saw the moon rise
for the first time in a dozen years.

And I had not heard of that man before his quick miracle
restored for him a world polished in new tears,
nor had I thought, since childhood,
of the seagrape tree I grew up with, never
imagining I would forget it
or that news of a miracle would restore it.

And what is the true nature of the miraculous?

Surely it is not science, arrived at by logic
and repeated demonstrations which would open
the unknown with the knock of a committee;
there's a cunning beyond such calculation
once the rationalist, vexed by paradox,
surrenders to the vision in a dream
and receives an image of the double helix.
The diamond that vanishes perfectly in water
reappears exactly when the thirsty man drinks.

2.

How young I must have been to
stand there
in the grasses
behind my parents' house
on the enormous spur of land
that is Florida,
         gazing up
into and out along
the great sinuous dance of those limbs, imagining
that they were wooden
extensions of the underground rivers
I had not believed in
before I turned the garden hose on full force
driving it nozzle-first
into the sandy earth
from which only neighbors,
            muttering and shaking their heads,
ever could haul it back up into sunlight.

3.

Out of that conjunction of my shadow and yours
                  and the trajectory of
the invisible river mercuric
underfoot,
underheart, you, tree of my youth, sprang
like an aorta of forked stone,
sprang gradually, gracefully,
                  a natural history of innocence
winding through blue air like the deep impulse you are,
an empire of songbirds,
and out along your vibrant limbs
                     I would climb
away from the earth, away from its underground

riddled with those inaudible waters troubling the sands
and ominously
constant, eating ground out from under my feet,
undermining that early faith in solid earth.

4.

What place could I dream of then able to withstand
the waters under the earth
suddenly real,
suddenly filled with images of a grey population
                of turtles, white-eyed garfish,
alligators ancient and goliath with milk quartz
installed in their blind skulls,
                a constellation of stiff bodies adrift
in those grim currents, pale and swollen, countless.

For this was the river of the kingdom of death and I knew
without being told
how deeply I and all living beings were involved;
that's when I turned
to you again, you
whose endless thirst rooted you in that abyss
but drawing up this darkness made it blossom into
                                foliage and song—
the same waters
that otherwise
would be sucking caskets clean. And I dared to tell no one
the contagion of that knowledge.

5.

So I climbed up into you
        and climbed until
                the highest breezes cleansed me,
taking refuge there among your thick queer leaves

where I could rock, singing
spirit songs any ear but yours would spoil,
clinging to the power of your limbs,
and they would sway
gently, bow
slowly under the swaying sun
whose broad light lay like insubstantial hands across my skin.

6.

In those sacred hours my songs were like the light
coming from everywhere at once
from the sun scattering your shadows
and from birds flittering
among your leaves
round like green ears all around me:
the red-winged blackbirds
like glimpses of distant fires at night,
the crowned blue jays, raucous,
tougher than the rest; the wild canaries darting among lemons,
the cardinals demure among the mangoes,
crows wisely gleaming, kingfishers and herons,
hoot-owls hooting in the hush of long nights
lit by the moonlike eyes of rabbits.

7.

And the magical knowledge of names!

When mourning doves mourned from the telephone lines
and mockingbirds startled me
with their perfect mockery
and whip-poor-wills cried their names over and over
from both thresholds of darkness so clearly
that I would go out to stand in the tangled fields, ecstatic,
then I began to hear meaning sing.

At night, late, when I was supposed to sleep,
I lay in bed, my chameleon
nestled along my nose,
his belly a horizon rising and falling
by one eye; sometimes
I lay there hearing you like a ghost at sea
                creaking and rustling
by the sleeping porch,
giving the winds
a body to whisper through; sometimes
when the house was still
I lay for hours, radio
held to my ear and tuned to Havana,
dim red tubes miraculously
wiring my skull with a language that sang
even without the music,
songs so quick my heart skipped beats to hear.

8.

I learned that even my homeplace, Florida,
sang with that tongue,
                sang "flowers,"
            sang tea-roses and hibiscus,
         sang jacaranda and gay bougainvillea
    sang day's-eye daisy and sword-of-the-gladiator gladiolus,
sang orchid double-rooted like the testicle, and tooth-of-the-lion
                                            dandelion,
sang honeysuckle from which we sipped the delicate sweetness,
sang croton and poinsettia, saffron crocus and rumpled
                                    elephant's-ears,
sang water-lilies afloat upon the waters,
sang seagrape trees.

9.

So this ancient man approaches you with his blinding years, daubs
his clouded eyes
with your clear pitch
... soon sees his own fingers crooked
tremulous and out of focus before his face,
and, as if for the first time, sees the delicately brimming
                    tissue of your skin wrinkled as his own,
your over-arching grace before the stiff Miami skyline.

And then the quizzical faces of strangers appear,
hearing this bent man groan
as old light scalds and fills his eyes again—
rumors of miracle are plucked from the charged air.

10.

Afflicted and desperate they come,
greedy and curious.
They approach you with prayers and wounds,
                    candles and demands,
hang medallions and rosaries from your branches,
smear their own gnarled limbs with your pitch,
strip your twigs and branches;
then comes night with more candles and pilgrims
impatient for another miracle.

At last the hour of the scavenger must come
in the uncandled darkness,
those drunkenly crashing and breaking your branches,
and then, with the morning star, the inevitable entrepreneur
—with the snarl of a chainsaw your trunk is gone.

At dawn
the blind remain blind, the deaf hear nothing.

11.

One day you are a tree merely,
          a mystery negligible in your ordinary loveliness,
your inauspicious appetite
drawing a self up out of the soil ignored underfoot.

The next you are a remedy
          for the blind and the lame, the endlessly wretched
who hunger for a cure
imitation can secure. They hack you to a stump.

Having healed one man
          you cure no more. Your true presence is untouched,
the luminous stigmata
of your pitch, stymied in the ascent up your ghost trunk,

blindly rises nonetheless, a flowing crown.
          A man inspired looks through his own eyes, sees;
the rest look for proofs first,
the rest look through ideas, remaining blind

to all the eye has seen.
          They reduce you to a tourist's curiosity.
Never have I known the green stone
of your fruit, opaque as milk, to be anything but bitter,

collapsing the cheeks of the wide-eyed
          and muting the fury of curses spat out with their pulp.
What is the nature of the miraculous?
Surely not event alone, surely a process rare in the witness as well.

12.

The blind remain blind, the deaf hear nothing.

But the old man, illiterate, whose tongue is the singing tongue,
has listened to the language
as a child,
as the blind man must listen, careful to detect the spell
 the see-grape tree, the see-grape tree!

And all of us are walking upon the waters under the earth.

For Miss Fanny Taylor of Fort Myers, Florida

My first full-fledged encounter with semiotics was all Walt Disney,
coming from Dumbo, the flying Elephant-boy with the ears
    like my own- - laughing stock ears that stuck out like suicide
car-doors flung wide on the highway, everyone pointing, pointing.
Except that no one pointed, only my dad, whose nose was such
    that he used it to keep a rainbow-billed toucan
out of the house when my mother wanted one, a touch of exotica
she could feed and befriend during those long afternoons
    she was forbidden to read. My father mistrusted books.

"One beak like this," he exclaimed, raising his face to the ceiling,
"is more than enough for any house." Of course I never guessed
    then what it was that a nose could stand for.
But Dumbo, I discovered, in the secret darkness of a matinee,
Dumbo could actually fly! I already knew how, unlikely as it seemed,
    according to engineers bumblebees couldn't fly
and I'd been stung often enough to grasp some fundamental flaws there,
so I watched his flights awestruck and hopeful and when he lost
    his feather at the top of the diving tower

I broke into a cold sweat. What could he do now! The feather drifted
down, down, swirling just as he had swirled, and the crowd
    roared for the fabulous Death-defying Leap
they'd paid good money for. And what happened next I'll never forget
because as we sat in the dark on a bright summer day in Florida
    late in the 40's, all of us white kids together,
it was Crows who came to the rescue, wise-cracking, jive ass Crows
whose jokes broke the mold of his fear, whose easy-going
    eye-rolling, loose-winged, bodacious daring

drew him off of his perch, dropped him, wide-eyed, into the abyss
of all that expectation, all that clamorous blood-minded cheering
    over which he was able to soar, victorious,
miraculous, while the Crows flew in unnoticed loops around him,

fetched him the feather and plucked it away, instructing him
      in a brotherhood few of us present understood
as we cheered for his victory, clapping for our familiar selves,
us with our oversized noses, wide-flung ears and freckles,
      fat butts and stutters, weeping mothers, drunken fathers,

not noticing, once we were out on the street, in the summer glare
of a Saturday we all just assumed then would go on forever,
      how there were no Crows in our part of town
where the paved streets were lined with grass and Royal Palms,
      no Crows in that theater we'd come from, none at the town
      fountain where we rinsed the popcorn shells from our mouths.
But that was the night when, as father pulled down over my ears
      the net he'd made of my mother's nylons, I remembered Fanny,
our Fanny, whispering, *Honey, don't you be so 'shamed—*
      God made those ears to notice what most folks won't never hear.

Misconceptions

Years back I heard mom explain
(I was just a kid)
her darkness to a nosy neighbor:
"Cherokee," she said.

And instantly my brave new blood
buzzed in its skindrum.
I rode my split-eyed pinto mare
bareback from then on

clinging with my thin young legs
to rib-curves slick with sweat.
We'd leap ditch after ditch,
long-knives in hot pursuit.

Preferring wilderness to town,
raw edges for horizon,
I worked to be a horseman
who wouldn't shame his kin.

I watched the weekend matinees
with a darker secret eye
trained to see betrayal glint
through eyes of cloudless sky.

I gazed in horror as Bob Hope
stacked fake Redskins high,
cringing as companions cheered
the acrobatic ways they'd die.

When Sons of the Pioneers would sing
I struck out for the snack bar
but when Cochise strode the screen
nothing could distract my stare.

I learned how water first would stretch,
then sunlight shrink a thong.
I knew how flickering tipis reeked
of horse-sweat all year long.

When bands of local Seminoles
came in from the Everglades
and gathered at the Dairy Queen
I'd look for moonbright blades

and when they shopped the A & P
each shy sound they made
I'd memorize the best I could.
Like quails clucking in shade.

I studied the shy women's skirts
with bands of handstitched colors,
the tight braids gleaming dark
above soft dazzling collars.

"Piss and bear-grease makes it shine"
I heard one man half-whisper
as wide-eyed ladies turned to fan
their cheeks, choke their laughter.

How simply innocence is taught
to mock another's ways.
Watching adults in the aisles
smirk and roll their eyes,

kids standing near faked warhoops,
or, half-stooped, danced in place.
One rolled his eyes, with fingers spread
mockingly behind his head.

Under attack, I stood as tall
as nine years let me stand,
proud of such sisters and brothers.
Each disfigured hand

was proof this one survived
his round with gators in a pit
we all knew busline tour groups
had paid to see them fight.

My heart, diverting from main roads,
had gone native for good
by the time I finally would learn
I had no Indian blood.

Crossing the Rez

for Joy Harjo

I was hitching a ride toward twilight
southeast of Billings, middle of November,
when a pickup let me toss my gear in back.
I climbed up into the cab boozy with two old boys,
Country Western AM blaring sad songs of love.
The driver's sidekick cackled "Cold enough out there
to chrome a bobcat's balls." He hoisted a pint of
high noon moonshine, shoved it into my chapped hands.
It purely thawed my tongue as they both jawboned
down the road, pointing out into the uniform blue dark
toward Custer's Last Stand. "Never trust no Injun,
bud, no matter *how* cold it gits," they soberly
advised, shaking their heads and slowing down,
dropping me off there, smack on the Rez, at sunset.

And there I stood the best part of a bad hour
until along came the first car that stopped,
a rumpled one-eyed station wagon, front bumper
dangling, muffler skidding ice-glazed blacktop
just like a kid's sparkler in the dark.

                                    "Hop in, par'ner,"
and in I hopped, stiff with cold, duffle on my lap,
all the wide dark faces, in front and back,
flat and friendly as old Hank Williams
carried on about good love gone bad again
from a scratchy speaker loose on the dash.
One popped the top on a Bud for me as gradually
we picked up speed, tranny wailing like a wolf,
everybody howling themselves into Hank's fix,
off-key and flat, while we hurtled through
the dark in a one-eyed comet.

"Where you headed?"
"Sheridan." He nodded, smiled.
"Thing is, par'ner, we can't take you there.
Off-rez cops, they catch us in this heap,
hey, it's bail-time in the Rockies. When
we drop you at Wyola, just
remember this: Cold as your ass gits
    don't park it in no cowboy pickup,
you'll do just fine. And do say howdy
for us In'dins to all the pretty girls
you meet on down the line."

Lodge Grass, Crow Reservation

The Snake Handler's Wife

On hard bleachers in an Arizona gym, she and I
        exchange glances and chitchat, discovering
we've both worked in Wyoming— she broke horses,
    I taught poetry. So we laugh, and she hands me
a rat snake as up front her husband arranges props
        while kids mill in like cattle for assembly.

Throughout the performance and display of vipers
        cooled and docile (and "Freddy" the python, draped
across the quaking shoulders of some poor
    English teacher speechless as the students squeal),
she remains impassive. Bored, I think, at first,
        as beside her I imagine countless times

she's seen this act, the myriad faces rapt
        above the sluggish boa in gyms from Casper
to El Paso, all rigid with the same fear,
    as he rattles off, in quick canned patter,
the chilling effects of constriction upon
        mammals of all sizes.... But no, that's not it.

She's simply been waiting. I watch her
        lips squeeze bloodless as her gaze
follows her husband to that odd huge basket
    draped in a green silk scarf. It starts to quake
and even the ratsnake she has let me hold
        — its tongue flickers, its the dull eyes stare—

perceptibly stiffens its chill in my hands.
     The scarf lifts, slips away. A dark wedge
weaving now at the wicker lip suddenly widens,
   dips shyly out of sight, rises again as he
darts and bobs, a tease, I finally realize,
       to draw it out for us— and out and out it comes,

its tall body delicate as wavering black flame,
     a quivering needle drawn by the attractive force
of his magnetic North. Even as the body arches
   the head, wide and slick as a wizard's hand,
counters swift as a laser. He dodges. Her
      hands have risen from her lap and hang in air

before her in the powerful attitude of a puppeteer,
     each encircling something invisible there
I gradually comprehend. It is as if
   each movement of the cobra plays like shadow
from those hands, as if by a remote electric will
      she can control each deviation of this force,

allowing it to turn and sway until some threat clenches
     both fists into radiance, each arm
locked stiff to hold it back,
   that blunt loaded chamber of a head,
while her husband— what a lucky man— drops
      the quenching silk upon it, bows for his applause.

Going My Way

I'd just finished
     matting that photo showing
     just how one-dimensional
the sorry houses passing for houses

on that sad street in Galveston were
     when there he was, out of
     nowhere, one arm hanging
at his side, the other waving, waving

like the vans on a dilapidated windmill
     catching that one last breeze,
     the blood slowly pooling
by one foot. He asked for a ride

knowing I knew he'd bloody up my car—
     asked hesitantly, but with
     just the degree of urgency
appropriate. I reached over

to help open the door. "How's
     it going?" he asked
     and I said "No complaints.
E.R. OK?" "No, man, no way,

I got no money, and that bitch
     didn't cut me half-bad.
     Not like my last wife."
I nodded agreeably and drove the mile

to the E.R. feeling like a hack-driver
      for some straight-back dignitary
      who wouldn't spend a single word more,
not for his life. I dropped him off in front and pulled out

quick enough to keep from having to explain myself
      to strangers. In the rear-view mirror
      I saw him raise up one hand, waving like
a fellow with a dozen fresh roses tucked under his other arm.

Strange Angel

Midnight in Grand Central
Is no place for an angel

And a woman underground,
Alone, is a bone soon found

Even in silence. But should
The found bone sing

In a place that cavernous,
Her earthy voice unearthly

As it turns vast stale silence
Into a duomo of Amazing Grace,

Then thank your lucky star.
Because such luck is rare: hers

For that voice so like the rustle of quills
In a widening wing; yours

For the normal blessing of ears
Crumpled and whorled for hearing.

If you approach her
Go with care. Caring.

She is not what she seems
If she is what she sings. Ears

Project a presence
From perfect vatic resonance

While eyes coolly discern
The grim cruciform

Of a female adult born
During the reign of thalidomide,

Her body bat-black and stub-winged,
Her pink lips cracked and swollen,

Her bright tongue archangelical,
Gaunt face drawn obsidian.

And this is how it is sometimes
Under the earth, at midnight,

Where we wait to be transported
By what we think we understand

From one place to another
While all we cannot comprehend

Gratuitously moves us through undriven mysteries.

Why I Remember

In memory of Bruce Elwin McGrew

> *Stories are like scars holding us to our wounds*
> *until we understand them well enough to heal*
> *whatever it is in us calling the enemy against us.*

1.

I charge these scrawls in a swelter of oils and turpentine
roiling through this studio lent by my old friend Bruce,
sizeable Scot I first met when he crept conspicuously
into the Sonoran auditorium where I was declaring

the storm of my early poems—him in his tartan kilts
and leopard skin, big bass drum and warrior's grin.
And still all these years later I will marvel at how
powerfully this beauty warrior's nuanced figures

reconfigure the old barnwalls—women of nubile light
mutable as clouds, shapeshifting fishmen,
aureolean chariot, bulls in sexual bloom—
while he's off sketching reflections from Lake Patzcuaro.

2.

Before heading out last night for another's reading,
I propped up your small watercolor of the coast at Moclips
remembering how I first saw that place March 1960
from a metallic blue, oil-spewing '52 Ford ragtop

out to escape my first and last formal philosophy class—
the T.A., pompous, logical, humorless and shrewd,
claimed Socrates was committed to suicide by "rules
as clear and binding as baseball's." I remember because

as the sun went down as it's going down in your painting
a car behind me came up flashing its lights and honking
until I pulled to the side. Two guys came up, got confused,
thought I was somebody else who drove a blue convertible

too fast with wild dark hair, then they asked me
back to see what they had in their car, and I,
because I was stupid, a couple years older, bored,
considerably more sober, I went, wondering what a pair

of Indian kids could want from me and too curious to resist.
When they opened the back door, there was their sister, they said,
and they kept mumbling something I kept not understanding
until one, reaching in, lifted her skirt. She stared up,

eyes out of focus, asking over and over "Whoozzis? Zisshim?
Who you toll me bout?" The boys, pulling Rainier beers
from their stash in a paper bag, offered me a can,
asked how much I had, asked if I

wanted a date with their sister, and she, reeking,
who couldn't quite sit up, was asking her question
over and over. Speechless, unnerved, I drove off
head whirling into the night, wondering what madness

in lives so young could drive them to this, lives
lived so far from the stupefying urban frenzy I'd
come here to escape, looking for nothing but a beach
to sleep on—top down to full moon and falling stars,

Socrates a renegade still alive and well in my heart,
radio crooning "All I have to do is dream, dream, dream,"
smells of surf and seaweed anchoring me to earth. So
I looked at your watercolor again—its ingenious beauty,

blue puddled on tan sand, water rising green, sky
a fan of gray and blue cut by streaks of raw salmon—,
and I remembered that girl, and I remembered the two boys
scarcely old enough to drive, all dying drunk, raven hair

blueblack in their faces, eyes darker than mine, bargaining
first for their sister and then for what was left
of their beer; and how beautiful that night had become
out under the stars, alone, the same stars those three

were born under, same sea they'd grown up hearing,
and I remember wondering what kind of dreams they
must keep sheathed sharp and deep in their hearts.
I was still wondering last night, driving into the city

to hear a Navajo poet read, just about the age
those boy's sister would be, if she lived—a poet
whose work I knew but wished to hear aloud myself,
30 years later. And I heard as she blessed her daughters

with first-day-of-spring and first-day-of-school songs,
heard her chide a friend for her "bad news" boyfriend,
a Navajo cowboy with raisin eyes and pointed boots.
I heard as she spoke of her own younger brother, dead,

buried, as she said, "in the strength of ageless songs,"
heard as she sang, beginning, "*Ashenee shishili*"
like the rustling of cornstalks just before rain,
ending, "It is as you predicted: we go on."

3.

When she pauses, looking up to whisper
in a voice as politic as silk rubbing silk, "This is
something we all know on Reservations,
but I don't think they tell you...." And she tells:
A young Navajo whose gas-pump jammed in Farmington
paid and started to drive off when through the rear window
he was shot dead by a clerk demanding 97 cents extra
"for the spill-over," a clerk later fined
for discharging a firearm within city limits
and fired for violating company policy.

                                  "Our lives," she croons,

"...not even worth a dollar."

4.

In the years since that night, I've thought, sometimes,
of that girl, thin legs spread like a child's
in the backseat, eyes muddled by beer and a future
incomprehensible at the time. And why I remember her

is not for an image lost in twilight but for the times
I've worried about her since then, whenever I see a woman
in that kind of trouble, with that kind of brother at hand.
And because I know such changes in fortune as I wish her

cannot simply be given, must be discovered—by luck, by faith
persevering but on a scale so hard for some to imagine
that their eyes extinguish waiting for some beacon
to shine from the horizon of their dreams.

5.

Dreams without friends who survive,
without even a common language
in which to aspire.... Of those most
gifted at survival, some few become

painters, say, or poets, glimpsing
a world's flawed heart in the mirror
of their own, giving the cunning of
their hands and tongues to those

from whom they learn to show not only
what it was like but what it was—
transfiguring paper into surf
we hear and smell standing there barefoot

where waves lapse into memory, turning
wandering pain into fixed constellations
where an orienting polestar stubbornly burns,
pulling us toward whatever it is our lives become.

Moclips, Washington

My Boots: Notes on Quality and Craft

1.

I choose the poorest shop, one far from the *zocalo*
where tourists like myself spoil things
for people like me.
                              For *los indigenos*—
who come down every morning from the clouds
through luminous mist heavy along paths
              feeding back roads from the mountains,
walking the dirt miles in from Zinicantan
              and San Juan de Chamula
with folded woven goods, *animalitos*
              and twiggy bundles of firewood
to set up shop by the cathedral—
for these people we are indispensable.
                              Ooohing and aaahing
we buy and buy, bracelets and blouses,
rugs and *rebozos, chiclettas* from the *chiquitas.*
Bargains for us are a living for them,
and trade is, as always, a fine excuse
to have a look at each other in the process.

2.

I bypass cobbler after cobbler,
peering in and inquiring
about prices while in truth
I'm keeping an eye out
for signs of the kind of poverty
I mean to lighten with my needs.

At last on a northwest corner
far from the rattle and blast of traffic,
I enter a cubicle dark and bare

as a monk's cell. No TV, no radio,
unplastered adobe. Here a rack
of handhewn planks stands empty
except for one pair of well-worn sandals
and another of skinny cats—
        one black, one calico—
neither much interested in a gringo
who carries his boots in a sack.

El viejo is blind in one moonpale eye,
just about as deaf as me, glancing up
from the bald tire he's carving a sole from,
squinting against the square of daylight
I've stepped in through. A small boy,
his grandson, indifferent as the cats,
spins a wooden top on the packed dirt
glancing sidelong to see if I watch.

3.

Six months later, back in the states
at a local mall in the Land of the Free
where I've hauled my boots in
to have the soles restitched: *Must be*
some butcher saw you coming
got the last laugh with these.

A fall and winter of the Eastern Seaboard's
acid rain and snow, and too much scuffling
on the sidewalks of Manhattan,
have chewed right through the cobbler's thread
and shrunk the leather just enough
to make repair here in Poughkeepsie
a major impossibility.
So I'll tell you what: I'm holding off until
I get into backcountry again, come summer,
when I'll find myself a shop far far

from malls and all their shining goods,
where a man with his grandson works on
through the years turning his eyes to moons,
a man who uses the hearing he's got left
listening to his grandson on the floor
singing snatches of tunes about revolution
and spinning his top in the packed dirt,
who keeps his one good eye on the stranger
who'll talk to the boy or not,
who'll spin that top with him or not.
And he will do the best job he knows how.

San Cristobal, Chiapas

Notice

"But you see, your *norteamericano* press reports
only massacres, not people killed."

So, mostly
they die in small numbers:

caught walking home
from one of the villages

alone. Or with a single companion.
Their faces, so broad and dark

and onyx eyed, their stature
so diminutive,

give them away. No one
but Indians walk here

so no one but Indians
get knocked to the ground

stripped, raped
as they pray in native tongues

incomprehensible to the ears
of uniformed strangers.

But once
when many died together

beaten down like stalks of maize
under a hail

of fresh hatred and ancient lead,
among the dead

was a young woman pregnant
with what—once

they had stripped her
to wash her for burial—

proved to be only
her husband's severed head.

Chiapas

Song from Chiapas

Whose eyes darkly gleaming
ever were so bright as these,
los ojos de los indios,
los niños de abajo

Marta and Victoria
of San Juan de Chamula
vye for our attentions
Comprar lo, comprar lo

We have no food for supper
no wood for the fire
our mother is too sick
to come to town today

Comprar lo, comprar lo
and dolls so like themselves
and bracelets quickly woven
promise colorful good fortune

Whose eyes darkly gleaming
ever were so bright as these,
los niños de los indios,
los ojos de los pobres?

When we treat these girls
to soup and bread, the gay
smiles of the girls outshine
the stony gaze of waiters

And once they realize
it's theirs to take, each
tucks away a slice of bread
for her hunger later.

Whose eyes darkly gleaming
ever were so bright as these,
los niños de los indios,
los ojos de abajo?

Who will feed them
when we're gone?
Who will buy *animalitos,*
who will buy them soup and bread?

And the bracelets quickly woven
that promise good fortune
and the dolls so like themselves—
Comprar lo, comprar lo?

Craft

for Jack Cady

Back at the rectangular harbor in Sitka
sheltered by its groins of stone,
mist, I knew, still would be rising
from spaces left by fishing boats
well before dawn, since this was
the annual one-day Halibut season
when men made or lost a fortune.
But just a hundred yards inland
among the looming Sitka Spruce
older than their namesake by
many centuries, there was sunlight
on the wood-carver's shoulder
and starlight in his voice.
He chanted one of the songs
of his people, over and over
under his breath. A song
for carving totems—for Wolf
and Raven, Eagle, Salmon—
a song for the carver carving.
The place was a native museum
where the carver wore jeans and
a flannel shirt, even a watch
"so I'll know when to break."
He answered several questions
during the casual half hour
before I asked if he ever tired
of carving the same traditional
totems over and over, if ever
he thought of starting one new.
The smell of cedar rose from
his blade, he smiled, the adze

raised a few more curls. "One day
a new dreamer will come among
the People—there will be fish
again, and game, and new stories
to show us once more a path
of light through the darkness.
Then, yes, there will be new totems.
Meanwhile," he said, resuming
his task, "we tread water,
we keep our tools sharp."

Translating Neruda

1.

Sometimes even when I sit with you
      —*diccionarios* and coffee,
               local ravens and sirens

     just outside
           under sun or stars—
               from everywhere I feel

   darkness pressing in again
            as I descend in that iron cage
                 through a shaft blasted into stone

    deep into earth with
           all the others I cannot see
                who cannot see each other.

2.

Near here, for money, years ago,
I worked in the big mine
        far below these hills of chaparral,
helping to render solid earth
        treacherous
with the hive of hollowed domes and shafts
        inhabited by laborers
who've known this life forever.
                Down there
only the young speak of love.
Those a little older boast of
"strange" and GTO's.

By thirty
they still speak lovingly of
their aging cars
        but payments
on the double-wide and doctors
for the wife and kids
        occupy their minds by then,
take their dreams hostage.

3.

The eldest, having learned
to take a certain delight
            from such darkness,
pride themselves on their skills
splitting stones with huge hammers
            in a single blow

while we newcomers with younger muscles
pounding   pounding   pounding
        end our first shifts
half-finished and done in.
While oldtimers under showers whistle
        we hoist our mud-caked gear

creaking up to the ceiling
on great gleaming treble hooks
                where hung like
            so many gutted miners
        by the next day everything's

        dried hard as bone.

4.

I remember at the end of each shift
that feeling
        as the man-train

brought us over dark rails through firedoor
      after huge firedoor, brought us in
      from the lines farthest out,
the places where no one would reach us if there was fire

back to the lift-cage rattling its half mile
          up the mainshaft, often in silence,
     as everyone prayed the cable would hold again
and suddenly
there was the world:
           desert bleached by sunlight,
        night sky opened wide by stars.

5.

Men die in such places,
as you well know.
        Some unbent, some broken,
falling into holes
they don't see
       and the holes they do.

And it was just such a place
    you came to,
       summoned
from the labyrinths
   of the written word
      by men black-faced,
black-lunged,
   eyes still
       fierce as fire.

And it was there,
    at the Lota coal mine,
       that you found

among the miners emerging
        that one—face disfigured by fatigue,
                        eyes blinking dust—
"rising as if out of hell"
        onto the fiery nitrate field,
                who extended his hand to you,
proclaiming
        "I have known you
                my brother, for a long time."

6.

When you died, Don Pablo, fearful for their own lives
people braved machine guns, defying visors
        black as insect eyes to march forbidden
through streets crying out your name, shouting
and calling out lines from your poems, singing
        down into the darkness of death to you,
hero of their love, hero of love's courage, you
who mined their hearts tirelessly your whole life,
        refining that ore into the airy gold of hope,
the only El Dorado real for them,
the only El Dorado that is real.

Laureate Proclamation

Mayor George Miller formally appointed William Pitt Root the first Poet Laureate of Tucson July 19, 1997.

Whereas Poetry, like rain in the desert, becomes most itself by giving itself away among the places where it is least known,

Whereas Poetry helps us realize we are bound humanly closer by our common interests than divided by our individual differences,

Whereas Poetry is a momentary stay against confusion,[1]

Whereas natural Poetry charges and recharges the surrounding ridges and arroyos of the Rincons and the Santa Ritas, the Tucsons and the Catalinas, and wishes to hear itself echoed from all that is human below,

Whereas in a community striving to maintain the brilliantly intricate tapestry of peace, Poetry is color-blind, knows no borders, shows that helping each other is one form of helping our selves,

Whereas Poetry gets straight to the heart of barrio and ghetto, ranch and rez, residential motels, trailer courts and the spillways of shade under shimmering freeways as well as to neighborhoods prosperously green all year and the gated communities of the foothills,

Whereas Poetry is bread as well as roses, fresh water as well as aged wine,

Whereas Poetry may strengthen the weak and injured, give recognition to the neglected and dignity to the afflicted, Poetry may also give the gift of affliction to those grown arrogantly careless in their strength,

Whereas old Ez declared "Journalism is history's first draft" and "Poetry is news that stays news",[2]

Whereas his pal, the good doctor, speaking of poetry, diagnosed how "Men die miserably every day for lack of what is found there",[3]

Whereas Poetry can go toe-to-toe with tejano, suit up for symphony, pop for hiphop, get real for rap, blow hot and cool for jazz, get down black for blues, lock into rock, match chicken scratch, even light that thing for good ol' country swing,

Whereas, even whispered, a syllable of truth commands more attention than a front-end loader full of the rubble and rubbish processed by spin-doctors,

Whereas prayersong is powerful medicine whose prescription hints we may all one day learn to Walk in Beauty,[4]

Whereas truth may thrive in the long nuances surrounding words just as songbirds survive among the cool blue spaces preserved among leaves at high noon,

Whereas some truths may be spoken while others need demonstration, so that there is poetry in rodeo both for rider and for bull, poetry in the mute glance of the Yaqui deer-dancer and in the shhh-shhh-shhh from the larval beads fastened to the hams and calves of those in the Easter procession; poetry in the dunk-shot, the touchdown and homerun; poetry in the drama of the grand gesture as well as in the genius of the unreported kindness;

Whereas there is poetry in all daily things well done,

Whereas "When power leads man toward arrogance, poetry reminds him of his limitations. When power narrows the areas of man's concern, poetry reminds him of the richness and diversity of experience. When power corrupts, poetry cleanses",[5]

Whereas Poetry is language dreaming a sacred pinup of its totally Rad, way Baaaaaaad self,

Whereas one poet says "Poetry makes nothing happen"[6] and another says "Poets are the unacknowledged legislators of the world,"[7] Walt Whitman, grinning broadly, roars, "Do I contradict myself? Very well then I contradict myself, (I am large, I contain multitudes),"

Whereas Poetry, like love, can be enjoyed before it is understood,[8]

Whereas it doesn't take a wizard to break the news that the world is at some times a Waste Land[9] and at others a Coney Island of the Mind[10] that can dizzy and bewilder us, or a Reality Sandwich full of seed syllables and Mind Breaths[11] that allows us to sound our barbaric yawps[12] and howl over the sleeping rooftops of the world,[13]

Whereas Poetry does, after all, render indelible witness to the otherwise unseen, unrecorded, the socially invisible, the culturally obscene, the mob scene, the all-too-cool, fobbed off discard of the mind's synaptic junkyard; to the last as to the first, to the worst as to the best; and to the thirst begun at birth through hungers blindly lunging toward the grave;

Whereas Poetry comes naturally from the mouths of the young, as when one child seeing a feather says "See, a bird flower!"[14] and another declares "A ruby is a drop of Eagle blood"[15]

Or

I used to be a door

but my parents slammed me shut—

Now I am a secret room, all lit up,

Waiting to be found[16]

Whereas Poetry *es una ganga por todos*—being priceless but costing nothing—and hence is a gift that taxes only the intelligence, that begs no more than heart and soul are willing to expend,[17]

$\mathcal{A}$nd whereas the Mayor, being a good sort, wants poetry on the lips of our city's citizens—its students, its lovers, its leaders, its dispossessed, impassioned, empowered—, its natives and its guests,

$\mathcal{T}$herefore does the Mayor of Tucson on this day[18] appoint William Pitt Root to be the first Poet Laureate of Tucson, a post created for a sequence of poets, each of whom, working in this unique capacity, even while acknowledging that we are all eternal mysteries briefly suspended in the passing solution of language, will endeavor to remind us of who we've been, who we are, and who we can become.

---

1. Robert Frost.

2. Ezra Pound.

3. William Carlos Williams.

4. From the "Navajo Dawn Chant".

5. John F. Kennedy.

6. W.H. Auden.

7. Percy Bysshe Shelley.

8. T.S. Eliot.

9. T.S. Eliot wrote *The Waste Land*.

10. Lawrence Ferlinghetti wrote *Coney Island of the Mind*.

11. Allen Ginsberg wrote *Reality Sandwiches* and *Mind Breaths*.

12. "Barbaric yawp" is Walt Whitman's description of the poetry to come.

13 Allen Ginsberg wrote "Howl".

14. Quoted from preschool daughter of poet Sandra McPherson.

15. Quoted from anonymous child in Idaho Poet-in-the-school program.

16. Quoted from anonymous child in Oregon poet-in the-school program.

17. Translation: "Poetry is a bargain, a good deal for everyone." A reassurance that the poet does understand that the position of Tucson Poet Laureate was created with a proviso that not one cent from tax monies would be diverted to support it.

18. July 19, 1997.

At the Feast of the Last Breath

For Tim, Without Whom

We first met at the backdoor when you knocked in the rain
looking for your high school friend since gone crazy,
the West Point washout who raced from Jesus and Mary
to Judaism then Viet Nam then came back with the pain

so common in those days, boasting of wasting kids
in one boozy breath, confessing he'd simply washed out
yet again in the next, sent home as a Section Eight
inveighing against the gooks, the niggers, and the yids

with the simple, disjunct insistence of the insane.
But he didn't come home that Sunday morning we waited
and chewed on Aquinas and Nietzsche and contemplated
each other in the gaps of our dialogue out of the rain.

Your impression, I gathered later, was that I was a brooder
and dangerous, but capable of the occasional phrase;
mine was that you were a tough guy, amusing, enormous—
Irish as Patty's own pig, and demonstrably cruder.

The years since then have rolled by in tides of wives,
our daughters washing up out of the surf like pearls
we've banked against emptiness in our scurrilous perilous
quests for respite, amid the riptides of our fluid lives.

Boy at the Black Window

for Tim and Maj and Doug Anderson

That boy you told me about
—you may not remember
but it sticks with me
like a burr
when I need it, when I
start taking the reins
too seriously.

Since then I've worked
with kids variously
"disturbed" myself: addicts
and alcoholics, runaways, delinquents—
an entire rainbow
of misery and anger.
Some of them are bright,
some dull, each one
poisoned on the way
by luck or love gone bad
until they just
won't show their passions
unless they're armed
with spikes or bottles,
guns or knives, tattoos
proclaiming FUCK THE WORLD
and NUMBER ONE FOREVER
The give-me-what-I-need's
that might be whispered
in a lover's ear
are snarled at a stranger
who trembles and complies,
hoping to live. Sad,

they are cruel; hopeless,
they crush hopes,
toy with dreams
private midnights disfigure
with nightmare.
                Together,
gradually, we enter
into the wilderness
of history and impulse
none would speak of
with me or the others
until we called it poetry,
and poetry it is
—language charged with
all the heart can bear.

Some wounds are so raw
they will not stop bleeding
until the relentless hope
that twists and turns
in them is broken. Others
dare to heal,
risking exposure. Some
write lines apt as knives,
deeply
and lovingly put
as any blade
in any gut, turned
into poetry
that must disrupt any
normal classroom hopelessly.

How do you begin again
with a boy, 10,
who writes
I used to be a door
but my parents slammed me shut.

Now I am a secret room
all lit up, waiting to be found
once his teacher says
"But real poems rhyme"?
Or the young woman, 15,
who begins
I am a vegetable
in the garden of death
after her teacher
tells her, "Honey,
didn't I assign
a poem in the shape
of a Christmas tree?"

I tell them how
"nice"
derives from "ignorance."
I tell them they
aren't nice,
they know too much,
and we go on from there.

And so it is sometimes
when I recall that incident
—how those neighbors
felt obliged
to have that boy committed
who, from time to time,
masturbated there
in his family's front window
and knew no better
and would not stop
and could not be permitted
to live on among them,
with their doors bolted
and their hearts withdrawn.

Who, exactly, was the genius
who divined
the final solution to it all,
and painted the lower half
of the tall front window
black, and saved that boy
with the remorseless grin
from his neighbors
and their scrupulous concern?

I think of him often.

                              Seattle

One Death of Li Po

After Wen-Ito

A pair of dragon candles burnt down to the quick
Stubbornly flickers on, cannibalizing wax tears
Shed once already as the guttering wicks cackle
Above a clarified pool wavering in the dark.

Half-heaped platters and drained goblets litter the table,
Wine jugs toppled as if out cold. The drunken guests
Long since have staggered home, scattering back to crows' nests.

Only Li Po, incredibly drunk, remains—slumped in a heap
            on a garden chair, chuckling,
Mumbling on and on, mangling whatever it is he whispers.

But his lips just won't stop moving, meshing inaudible syllables.

His eyes, each a drunk dwarfish and bloated, bulge abruptly,
Held back by their red webs; they blaze forth
Brazenly at a single timid flame before him
And he is as a ravenous lion crouching over its prey.
Two golden eyes silently transfix it.
He lifts one forepaw, softly, softly
Like light intuiting light, and springs....Platters, candles
And goblets from everywhere crash, clatter, clang,
Pulled down by his sudden lunge
                        utterly out of this world.

At the Feast of the Last Breath

for Tim and Hannah Riley

Unavoidably, there turned the poor young thing sprigged and
        tastily spitted
above hot coals where we all sat, chattering, as it hissed,

spattered and seared golden as you kept everyone
in stitches with the wicked lampoons and loopy wry asides

that could've brought an army of unBelievers to their knees
(or brought on an army of Believers, hood-headed, with torches),

serving up skewered stupidities of the left, the righteous,
and the lukewarm in Gatling fashion, a Confucian hitman—

a deadly prelude to a feast had the slaughter not amused us. Yes,
I write, but it's you who are true laureate of all things hapless,

armed to the gills with prickly wit, unbeaten heart, and pointy quills
loosed straight to their marks, all Dicks and Bloody Mary's.

And then after the feast and after Burt's wife rose and danced
among the demolition of bones and bottles on the wet tabletop,

after the thanks belched from all quarters of the deck and dark
and the sleepy nods of infants in arms, and the stoned snarls

of couples still at odds over who'd been with whom in the can,
and the TV's neon flaring in the living room, and the cat the cat—

the cat you catapulted cart-wheeling toward the Milky Way...
then the yowling guests started leaving. Friends from work,

friends strictly from hunger, friends no one's ever seen before
with lamb ribs and silver poking out of their holey wife-beaters,

aging bikers with spiders webbing their bare skulls blue,
biker chicks with stretch-marked butterflies fluttering,

punks with their pierced lips, shrinks with piercing glances,
all gone. All. All but the cat, who crept back in from the night

unrepentant and unharmed, alert and curious, curling up just where
you lay your shaggy story-roaring down, on folded forearms, purring.

I remember your last lamb roast for young Hannah,
how you watched a young moon dance on the ancient waters.

The Lord's Work:
Snatch from a Waking Dream Brother Tim
Shared with Me the Day Before His Funeral

So then she looks at me
        & blinks
& looks away
        you know the look
& looks at me again
        & says "Sooo, Mr. Riley,
just what are
        your plans?
For your life, I mean,"
        she adds,
adenoidally,
        as if trying
to correct
        something.

Mind you, Willy,
        I'm there to get advice
on what to do about
        that income tax
I haven't filed for 10,
        12 years,
intending never to.
        But their letters kept
piling up. And then
        they said
We'll take
        your house away.
My everything
        that can be carted out
or auctioned off.

            I hadn't thought
I'd live so long
            and now
I'm here
            to see what
I can do,
            short of dying,
to keep some something
            to pass along
to the girls. Who,
            mostly,
do not need it.
            But I need
it to give.

& so
            & soo
& soooo
            I tell the nice lady,
who sharpens & brightens
            the teeth in her grin
on back taxes, this:
            It's like with leaves
I've always liked
            watching leaves fall
just sliding through
            the air, tossed up
& down, circling,
            until they land
on earth
            then rain
washes them
            down hill
& maybe there's a stream
            & maybe there's a river
& you know how it goes,
            without intention,

with only this
        drift of wind
or that
        twist in a current
so it turns,
        turns back,
turns again
        & (you guessed it!)
just goes
        on and on...
until it gets
        there.

I nod, scratch
        my nose, nod.
"So that's my
        life plan.
Such as.
        My life plan.
Is." She
        looks away
again,
        purses
her withered lips,
        sets down her pen.
"I just don't
        know what I
—what anyone—
        can do for you."

Walla Walla

On Learning a Friend's Name
May Now Be Added to the Quilt

In Memory of Bob Mony

Foregoing, by way of burlesque, whatever may've tempted us
toward the tragic—that was your early style, the one
by which I knew you first, and best, three decades back
when we were all still undergrads, ill-defined. Red-haired,
freckled, with specs and a ready wit, you were, as friend Tim
put it, "a tad light in the loafers," yet so ferociously intent
when you crouched hovering over the glowing keyboard,
you electrified your friends, straight and gay alike.
Classical thunder that broke from your flashing hands
sustained the fire steady in your eyes through long nights
we all spent in the haze of the Blue Moon Tavern, laughing.
I remember when your friend, Joel, took to his bed
playing Deborah Kerr to your hilarious Yul Brynner,
how you were mortified by your sheer delight. Then
when he left for Paris, apprentice to a master pianist,
all of us were envious. Somebody's life was taking off!
We were left on the dock, waving, helplessly ourselves,
our dreams overshadowed by another's actual feat.
How many years did you spend then as hired accompanist
invisible to thundering phalanxes of beginning dancers before
you took to bodybuilding, bulking up your scrawny frame
so much I'd never have known you on the street?

                              All I did know came from Tim,
who told me, told me just today, over his blurred breakfast
of shotgunned triple bourbons, that yesterday you died. Blurted it
because there was no other way to say it. And so, I realized,
you'd died in Manhattan during an eclipse of the full moon.
And someone who'd caught your pioneering TV spot for AIDS
paid your way, just in time, for two last weeks of King's X

in exotic Hawaii—"home to more endangered species
than anywhere else on earth." Gentle-hearted, wry, so rare,
you were one of the good guys, a lover of poetry, music,
and wit honed to an edge so fine a victim hardly knew
the necklace of blood at his throat was his own.
                                                    So, if
I say your life has had its own modern fairy-tale ending,
registering the grim mystery in your own droll key, I trust
you would approve. May you sleep well, brother Mony,
and by flawless music be relieved of all your dreams.

                         Gig Harbor

"We Must Take Care of Our Monsters"

Written in Bruce's Studio at Rancho Linda Vista

1.

Tonight, midnight, outside it's all stars
and moonless desert hills. Inside,
your stereo belts out Hound Dog Taylor's
roadhouse blues behind the revved up squeak
of old Possum reading (I'm taping "Four Quartets"
fast-dub on my old totable black boombox.)
All the while I eye your latest canvas.
Each year you make a new community
of images evolving the commonplace
to such an irresistibly mythic pitch
my poor dry tongue feels counterfeit
before them. Like the women in them
they elude the currency of easy praise.

2.

Earlier, on my way down through the wash
from house to here, I trundled along carefully,
coffee in one hand, Oscar Wild tugging his leash
wrapped round lunging flashlight in the other.
I walked tenderly barefoot on the grit still damp
from our afternoon monsoon, cooling down sand
for annual tarantulas and perennial rattlers,
my fellow nocturnals. The veering flashlight
cast Oscar's Neanderthal shadow huge
across the flashing path. That's when I
noticed how such a shadow as any of us casts
could've easily concealed the fist-sized spider
I'd picked up to study under a magnifying glass
before I put it back in the wash:

So delicate are these pelted monsters
that a simple drop from a tabletop
cracks one like an egg. What care
we must take of our monsters, my friend!
That same shadow could conceal the diamondback
or sidewinder who print the sand each night
with their hieroglyphic comings and goings.

3.

Having switched hands to steady the light,
better to choose my way, I noticed
how the sacred *d'aturas* climbing the stairs
to your studio had slowly folded closed.
No moon.
            Always on the chrome nights
of a summer moon, they broadcast
with their wide white crumpled trumpets
a cool mantra of seductively insidious scent.
I smile remembering a few years back you told me,
having smoked one, "Time...
ground to a halt." As your hand waved off
gracefully into emptiness, you grinned.

4.

And now here it is on canvas before me—*d'atura*
not quite a *d'atura* facing a figure not quite
a two-headed serpent and not quite a stone tree
while a white-eared cottontail hops away
from an angel-hair cactus caught up in its
crown-cocoon of thorns. Just off-center
a *brujo* (or a blue-hooded stone like a *brujo*)
is backed by shadows on the living path
as a boy pulls bark back from a downed tree...

or is it a mischievous angel lifting the door
at the top of the skull, peering
curiously in at another word,
catching the likeness of what you've seen
that has no likeness, quite, upon this earth?

Being Moved

In Memoriam: Bruce Elwin McGrew, a true Scot Beauty Warrior

One day, after shifting from railed bed
        to rickety folding wheelchair en route
to another CatScan, you sat there yellow, gaunt, and drawn,
        tubes and cords lolling down and wrapped round your arms and ankles,
bereft of any shred of what we think of as dignity.

Ed and Pam and Fox and I were glancing sidelong at each other
        —What can we say? What can we do?—
when in came a new nurse to make up your bed. She ignored "the patient," you,
        until your shaggy right eyebrow shot up,
you smiled a longtoothed smile, softly coughed on the back of your hand,

then gestured, with such elegance, for her, to the tubes and disarray:
        "All this, " you confided, "is just an act."
You know the voice you used. She stared, she started to laugh, she
        started growing beautiful again as she pulled back the sheets.
We were laughing too, wiping at our eyes with the backs of our hands,

And when the ones all in white wheeled you out,
        the look on that bearded face of yours
reminded me of a long-eared hound
        crouched in the back of a battered pickup
pulling out onto the freeway at last, face set into the rising wind.

Ballad of the Guys I Knew

Friends? Hell, all we got in common is a ex-wife or two.

The thing about the guys I knew
they all enjoyed their fun
they'd party till the moon turned blue
grand boozers every one

They'd party till the moon turned blue
and roar at jokes and sing
fall in love and out of love
as if it were a swing

fall in love and out of love
and promise anything
and wake at dawn on the move
before alarms could ring

and wake at dawn on the move
to jobs that drained them dry
and left them with a quenchless love
of whiskey, gin, and rye

and left them with a quenchless love
of speed, fast cars and women
traded in each year to prove
their lives weren't slowing down

traded in each year to prove
they still had what it takes
to play the games of cash and love
and keep raising the stakes

to play the games of cash and love
and take it on the wing
With each night longer than the last
the same old jokes grow boring

With each night longer than the last
and booze and pills for sleeping
the guys for whom life was a feast
could feel their handholds slipping

the guys for whom life was a feast
found their tables bare
and on their tongues the bitter taste
of famine for a future

and on their tongues the bitter taste
of tares planted in spring
of summer joys laid to waste
and thistles fiercely bristling

The thing about the guys I knew
they all enjoyed their fun
they partied till the moon burned blue
and turned each one to stone

Neither Basalt Ledge nor Turnip,

or:

Fields and Forests

Illustration by Albert Kogel.

Query for Owl at Spring Equinox

Rainpocks in
old snow
            black twigs
drenched
            in lunar sheen.

Owl, from what perch tonight,
claw-clenched,
rinsed in drizzle,
will you drift that haggard single vowel
you've stolen from the moon?

Whichever humdrum suburb
you haunt,
            your autumnal
presence—reminiscent of dry leaves
and warm fur twitching
in your grasp—
will occupy innumerable dreams
with grim wonder
as you cry your muted cry across the sleepers.

Puffed up like some Diogenes
overly aware
            of your familiar errand,
your fingers gone to claws
on this endless quest,
your ancient eyes
            lamps of their own,

you know perfectly well
　　　　we who begin as dreamers
close our lives
in sleep
and yet on those lips of horn
always the same question
asked in the same key.

Yours is the angelic race
from reptiles evolved,
winged raptors conjured
out of subtle cunning
and its curse.
　　　　　　　From which
of the mineral-eyed
have you arisen, your scales
elongated into quills, your head
great as the moon
now warm-blooded in you, ravenous
for an answer to your query,
the insatiable rhetoric
of your unwringable neck?

Only your
dry tongue, exposed
as you hiss
at us, hints
of your origin.

I ask you, Owl,
ask you
as new rain falls
on old snowpack
beneath twigs shrunken dark:

How far have you come?

How far do you mean to go?

New Paltz

Most Likely

for Peter Warshall, beloved,
in Paradise before us

Outside
In the dark dark only
Because I haven't got owl's eyes,
Accumulating waves arch, crashing
Across sand I suppose
Isn't aware of them.
                              Queen Anne's Lace
Along the ridges probably can register
By its own clock the dilations
Of stars my eyes could never guess.

It isn't life that's strange.
What's strange
Is the assumption
We know enough
To know what strange would be.

I am, as we like to put it, everything
I've been en route to all I will become,
Halted, for these few unstable years,
In this form
Neither basalt ledge nor turnip,
Seal whisker nor cloud.

                         Bolinas

One for the Climbers at Shawangunk Ridge

in memory of Haig and Regina Sherkerjian, their love

Lying by the lake imitating twilight
as an old man and woman canoeing near shore
fish among grey clouds, I drift among
the clouds lit within myself by desire,
long banked, long neglected, until,
lids sliding open, closed, I realize how
tenuous the power is that lets us live—
little more, at times, than surface tension
in the lake where just so long as calm prevails
images are perfect. And yet it's never long
before some breeze must come to roughen up
the shimmer of raw wonder, leaving water
water once again, as some disturbance,
natural as wind, must come even to dreams,
startling that subtle membrane between
long sleep and the waking to find dust
is dust again, the lids profoundly sealed.
And thinking this I open my eyes wide.
The couple's gone, the clouds tarnished and dark,
and somewhere far above me, among the cliffs,
I hear directions being shouted by the climbers
one to another and laughter from these youths
secured by faith to risk, by steel to stone.

Sparkling Ridge Road

From One Old Dog to Another

In Memoriam: each and every sweet one of our wildlings

With even a casual glance into your eyes
I've seen light deep as the bones of my body
glow back out at me, your tongue

a pure pink joy hanging lathered and wide;
your heart so powerful it leaps like a rabbit baffled by your ribs
thumps under my hand.

        With you I regained from my youth knowledge of raw delight
                gradually supplanted, put to sleep year by gray year,
                                habit by habit.

      Even our nights run parallel: Until I lay the dog of my body down
           you remain beside me, flopping curled at my feet when I sit,
                            rising when I rise,

eyes upon me always, even while I mull the dull leafy white meals
I hold between us, the books you sometimes sniff,
puzzled. And when I flop

before TV, on the black beanbag you claim for you own
in all the intervals, you slink slyly behind the set itself,
to lie in my line of vision

        during the hours actors manufacture lives of moving light—
           your head resting on a stuffed toy, until I snap the TV off
                              and wake

      back to our life, tossing you the belled lamb you quickly, gently
           snatch from air before it hits the floor, your eyes brighter
                       than most human laughter. Once

I finally join our Pam in the bedroom, within seconds you're
beside us in the dark, at your own inalienable post
facing the door, guarding our sleep.

Now and then I've been wakened from nightmare by your nose
in my face and I've heard you, as well, whimpering in terror,
felt your legs, dream-bound, twitch.

> Placing my human hand on your inhuman trembling face,
> I've felt the muscles anchoring your jaws soften,
> I've seen your eyes opening

> go easy with that ancient glow in which I recognize myself,
> and I've known things man alone
> cannot hope to know.

To the Wolves at My Door:
An Apology of Sorts

for Lulu and for Haps

While I type
      in she trots
            out of open daylight,

a hundred pounds of girl wolf,
      her laser-gaze golden,
            her soft ears half cocked.

When I lean down
      to rub muzzles with her,
            sandgrains on her chin

give her away:
      She's been
            in the garden again,

devotedly burying bones
      or digging them up,
            and now she's smuggled

into the study
      with all its musty books
            the stuff of fields and forests,

the odor of
      earth freshly stirred,
            in a word

fertile ground!
      Bless you,
            Lulu *garou*

you've done the work
cut out for you.
Now let me do mine.

A Flower of Human Light

Illustration by Albert Kogel.

Love Runes

How odd, how interesting, what a blessing
that skin behaves
       as skin does
touching other skin,
that lips skimming
       fingertips draw
lips to themselves, as

a droplet on a green leaf
touching another gathers up
       substance and courage
to merge yet again,
the lens it forms enlarging
       what it rolls across
for special scrutiny, each vein and pore

just for that instant
a pure revelation, the
       uniqueness
fleeting yet impressed
perhaps forever
       like a certain kiss, like
the scent-print pit-vipers

mark in ill-lit, labyrinthine brains
as a clue of spark
       once they've struck
living flesh, taking
into the mucous lining
       of expanding jaws
the single molecular particle

of spoor required to guide
a serpent's tongue
            to its stricken quarry—
the ruby-eyed sweating toad,
the panting rabbit—
            until it drops. Love,
if it runs true

to form, similarly draws
what is unique
            into gentle jaws
softened by such elastic lips
and irresistible hisses
            that the ones struck recoil,
inevitably, in wonder

at its subtle power to disarm
so utterly—predigesting
            all objections
like bone chips
or bits of skin, so
            that the two are one,
Ourobouros, before the spell is done.

A Gift of Stone

Bending over the pond's surface
we see ourselves looking up
out of the sky behind us

where clouds have gathered
like the faces of ancestors
in a high memory of wind

while we muse in silence
looking into this mirror,
looking out as we look in.

And when you reach a hand
down through the clouds
to lift from the bottom

a stone, as a gift for me,
it is a gift from ancestors
who reinforce your gaze

with generations of dreams
brought to such fine focus
in your eyes, how could I refuse?

Another Note

This is just to say
I have eaten
you before
and will and will

again while you
make summer
lunch in a short
skirt the wind

of my brown hands
lifts gently up
to show
the white rump

not of antelope
though the floor
will rumble with
the clatter of hooves

Ode to a Russian Blonde
Who, Before Sleeping, Wishes Someone Might
Write Her A Poem Before She Wakes

I would pity the blind
who will never
dazzle in the fair fire
of your Russian hair,
          except
that they may know you
by the fountain
of your leaping voice,
the graceful flight
of your excitement.

I would pity the deaf
blind to
your voice,
          except
that with their eyes
they have such access
to those delicately
soaring hands
you speak with
and to the tender
brilliance of
hair you sweep
from eyes
blue as the sun
to those
you look upon.

Then I would apply
my pity to
companions too distant
to see you
go about the dailiness
of living like
a flame innocent
of the light and warmth
it shares merely by being
what it is,
              except
that even they
have memory
to know you by.

Finally then,
I will pity those
who know you now
only by this poem,
hopelessly aware that
they must live out
their remaining lives
tantalized by the bare
possibility
of a chance encounter
with such a one,
whose very name
means
whence the honey flows,
that cataract
of sweetest light
by which,
as you sleep,
I write.

                              Oklahoma City

Desert Walk After Rain, After Love

Night—stitched and bound
    by fire
  zigzagging through
    desert rain—

turns to morning,
    opens like
  a book
    publishing light.

We walk out
    glad to be here,
  recharged in lucent air
    healing with

mesquite and creosote,
    cat's-claw
  and Palo Verde. Each
    specie,

armored with
    thick skin or thorns
  fierce against
    any flesh,

unfurls against extinction
    rugged blossoms whose
  crumpled translucence
    is the proud brilliance

of a thousand nations
    broadcasting their wealth,

the scent of their riches
     set adrift

to guide armadas of
          humming bees and cackling
barbarian hordes of birds
          to rummage and pillage

around the heart
          of each calyx
sweet, seeded fruits
          and puffs of pollen.

And here on a rise squats a barrel cactus,
monstrous anemone affixed

to the desert floor of this ghost-ocean,
sunlight gleaming on the pale green skin

suffused with rich milkiness,
smooth surface ridged with rows of hooks.

To glance into the thick-petalled center
of such symmetry and succulence

is to be drawn into the gaze
of a splayed radiance

replicating flame in a frozen attitude
warm as the wax of a candle

whose wick still glows
where extinguished lovers lie

with the glister of salts drying on lips and thighs,
happily breathing each other's breath.

For the blossom is wholly sexual,
vegetal desire's signal fire

bright as the scent of the luna moth
luring her partners from miles off,

blood-crisp crimson, irresistible orange,
saffron fit for bedding a king;

and the textures are sexual textures,
silky and slick, glistening,

open to sun,
moon and stars, inexhaustible avatars

for all who give themselves to darkness
while yearning for the light.

Tonight as I
lie beside my wife, quilts thrown back,

I'm watching moonlight recreate her shape
in the lustrous figure

of a flower of human light, whose delicate center
still vividly trembles at the tip of my tongue.

Rancho Linda Vista, Oracle

This Kiss

Now you are sleeping, voyager beyond
empty realms, afloat
upon your own luminous energies

and I am preparing for the voyage
Neruda called
the poet's one sacred duty—*To leave*

and to return. But first,
I must finish this kiss
to leave with you,

this brush across your lips in darkness
churning with
uncommon dreams, our common journey.

                                        En route

Stewe + Ingela, Ingela + Stewe

The day we arrive, in rain, from our far distant continent,
      Ingela, new love of my old friend,
having already gathered an armful of wildflowers for my wife
      suddenly remembers me as well and steps out of her clothes
into the mirroring midsummer Swedish waters to retrieve this
      long-stemmed lily she places, dangling like a garland,
around my transcontinental neck
      the moment I pass through customs,
the instant we arrive.

Keep her, my friend. Be kept by her.

Kungälv/Göteborg

Among Fools,
Soothsayers
and Rings

Illustration by Albert Kogel.

Classical Figures

You must change your life. So says the poet
speaking for the headless torso of Apollo
whose every sparkling curve
      some anonymously human hand
      relieved from stone
so long ago. Just who quarried that marble
from Paros or Carrara, and under whose whip
      or wage, we'll never know.

And yet some mountain was partially dismantled,
some roadbed groaned under the sagging wagon,
and coins were exchanged
      again and again in
      several denominations
before the first blow of mallet upon chisel
alerted the old god locked within
      that soon light was to break again

upon his careless brow, where curls would reassemble
and the eyes like spectral apples glow.
What thoughts took shape
      in the temple smoothed
      by the rasp
once skilled mortal intention
rendered stone divine? And what curious rhetoric
permits such a question, as solvent among fools
      as soothsayers and kings?

Nor can we tell now by the look he gives,
for having lost his head to some barbaric impulse
in our stricken past, he stands aloof, noble
      upon a pedestal,
      each limb a fixture

fluent as the wind, each joint a semblance
of articulation, this knotted frame of being
 once stone, now rippling flame.

When Rilke stood before him—Rilke who would die
blackened by infection taken from the rose
 whose image meant
 the world to him—,
stood like a vessel poised to take
the tide instrumental to an ancient force,
 somehow Apollo opened

eyes of stone and looking through
the poet's mortal eyes
 saw his own immortal face
 appear as fire in air,
and so spoke a last time, saying
the one thing gods say to mortals
 which is always true.

 Pietrasanta, Tuscany

Conversions for a King

After Kierkegaard

Because he has spoken freely in the land of a King,
because he has offended a King,
royal smiths are fashioning for him this huge brazen bull,
crafted ingeniously to contain on the beaten floor of its belly,
above that gradual fire the King's own hand shall set,
this one man, naked, crouching.

                        A hollow
instrumental to the man's breathing
will wind through the monstrous throat
where it must further serve to flute
the bitter cries of his long burning
through lengths of gold and silver
so subtly turned, so torturously tuned
that of such cries
is made the sweetest music.

                  Strip him.
Give him to the Bull. The king tonight
is restless and would warm his hands
at the fire and by the conversions
of an enemy be soothed.

Mousehole, Cornwall

The Poet in Polite Society

Baudelaire it was who drew the poet out
as albatross—great ungainly bird
burdened with wings that might, unsummoned, sprout
at any moment from his hump, unnaturally absurd
appendages for any man to bear
who meant to be mere mortal among mortals
and not an awkward shade among the fair
est of the fair, with their preference for Normals.

His open collar, rolled-up sleeves, clear eye
betoken his healthy willingness to frolick....
but such would-be otters as are born platypi
have little choice about it: Frau Luck
has tossed the fatal dice and, laugh or cry,
the Poet must be quick to learn the social Tuck.

Montmarte, Paris

Cat in the Workshop

The cat, like that,
came through
      the open door

where we were
writing poems
      of love, .

yowled once
& yowled again,
      rubbing her

yellow-eyed
menagerie of appetites
      against the pillar

holding up
the roof over our heads
      till out

we tossed her,
this urine–eyed monster
      who mocked our

talk of assonance
& passion, our
      pallid impressions

of her hot raw
vowel-howling,
      her hungers

purred in thunder
mere disturbances
       to us

who scratched
at silence
      with our earnest pens.

              Winston-Salem

With Luck:
Wrapping Up After a Writer's Conference on Puget Sound

After the last of the readings,
I've come back to my room
to look out at the simple dark
and sit in the window, reflecting

on your pumpkin cat—
How her eyes vivid as moons
shine while she watches
from her perch on your window

the puppetlike swallows
swung as if on strings
back and forth between
your eves and the world,

bearing the grubs and worms
their brightbeaked young
bury their heads in those mouths
to devour, bald heads like tiny buds

bulging over the thatched edge
they'll probably fall into flight from
before the next rent is due.
With luck

and the right timing
they'll make it and your Phoebe,
grown wiser but no fatter,
will crouch on the sill—trembling

tail tip twitching out of control,
her birdcalling song blooming
like a dry stalk from her throat
as she strangles on desire,

her choked voice transformed
by sheerest concentration into such
a likeness of the swallow's chirp
that I, though I know better,

stare in awe at her, half convinced
that she has in her mouth, carefully cradled,
one of their fallen bodies,
that out of her jaws are peering

small eyes bright as driven nails
and that at any instant now
one of those perfect chirps
will pull out behind it

a half grown swallow suddenly
graceful enough to fly free
of that unlikely carnivorous nest
which is Phoebe's mouth.

But no bird sings
there in that dark
—only hunger raised to such a pitch
that Phoebe's eyes shine

like false landing lights
as her jaws drip and delicately foam.
Raw desire bright as a mirror
in her heart

has conferred upon her
the power almost perfectly to mock
the swallow's song,
though any swallow knows

swallows only sing that song in flight.
Across the empty fields
lights in the students' rooms burn
late into the night

where young poets, hungry
for worlds of their own invention,
devise their power songs
and perch prepared to soar

over nests of jaws
waiting for them at home
singing the songs of habit
which lure the weakest down

but will fail to deceive
those who know now
only the song sung on the wing
is the voice of an honest god.

Port Townsend

To a Wasp, Crawling
Over the Desk in My Study, Late

After a night grading papers,
Facing a whole day of teaching,
I know the feeling, old fellow—
Encasement in aging armor

And wings once invisibly vibrant
Now just a bit theatrical,
Still held aloft but stiffening
Like pages from some old tome.

All six legs still function,
And Lord know how many eyes
Useless in such enclosed spaces—
Though the stinger inspires respect—,

And I think of Toshira Mifune
In his leather Samurai gear
After a few too many *sakès*
Over a few too many years

Hauling himself up again at dawn
Erect as an insect, authentic
In each expression that crosses
His absolutely professional face

While one-eyed cameras roll
As the bloody sun continues to rise
And we stare over buttered popcorn
And I stare, poised at my keyboard,

And students stare, taking down notes,
At the hung-over warrior about to act,
At the staggering wasp struggling to fly,
At the hired poet about to try to explain.

Red Mills Road, New Paltz

Calling the World to Order

I sing of the rooster's armored legs
and eyes crazed wide by sunrise
and that comb, hot and red,
flopping as he cocks his absurd gaze

and takes into each eye the charge of light
and grips the top rail with his horny grip
as, calling the world to order,
he makes each thresholding star tremble in the sky.

What poet dares with indifference to behold him,
those lyrics edgy as iron, lucid as ice,
that ruthless blood-tongued cry
drawn from a throat sheathed in rainbows of the living flame?

Albion, California

7 for a Magician

In memory of Ray and Miriam Rice

> *"To create moon*
> *in one's self"*
> —Ouspensky

1.

Out of his black hat
he draws
rabbit after rabbit

and out
of the clear air
breath after breath.

2.

It takes him years
to learn
perfectly the poise
with which to reach
into his own sleeve,
withdrawing
the blaze of silk
it takes a generation
of mulberry leaves
and worms to spin
and the fingers
of strangers
to weave.

For the magician
about to astound
his audience.

For the lady
about to betray
her lover.

For the matador
into whose unborn wounds
first the horns
and scarlet scarf
then the faithful worm
must pass.

Applause.

He bows.

Applause.

She cries out
to the dark.

Applause.

His eyes widen
as the horn sinks in
and in.

3.

Who brushes
the magician's favorite hat?

The rabbit and the dove.

While he tends
to the hutch and scattered nest.

4.

His best makeup
is in our minds,
the hunger
of old locks,
rusted and lost,
to be opened.

Even skepticism
is a prayer
to him,
for whom fire obeys
the moon,
for whom water burns.

Imagine
the key of ice
designed to enter stone,
the lock made of mercury
which is its own pure key.

And look
into the clarified eyes
of just this one
who performs dreams,
who never sleeps.

5.

He brushes his teeth,
blows his nose,
eats with his mouth,
has but one suit of clothes.

He is very much like us,
it would seem,
to us.

6.

After each performance
he disappears.

Outside the stars brighten,
inside
the lights go on.

On the other side of the earth
it is morning
where he shares breakfast
with the chimpanzee,
who asks if it all went well.

And they laugh as they eat.

7.

The last achievement
of an ultimate magician
is the proper
care and treatment
of all beings
filling the vast emptiness
of that hat
with which he lives.

Crotty House, Chapman's Point, Mendocino

Acknowledgments

Thanks to the following periodicals and anthologies where some of the poems in this book have first appeared: *Asheville Poetry Review, Best of Southern Poetry Review, Best of Cream City Review, Comeback Wolves: Western Writers Welcome the Wolf Home, Commonweal, Cream City Review, Dogs Singing: A Tribute, The Ecopoetry Anthology, Georgia Review, Helicon (Israel), Harper's, High Plains Literary Review, The Lucid Stone, Malahat Review (Canada), Manōa, Many Mountains Moving, Mesilla Press, Niederngasse, New Millenium Writings, New Poets of the American West, Nimrod, Olive Tree Review, Poetry (Chicago), Poetry Miscellany, Poetry Northwest, Poets Respond to SB 1070, Rattapallax, San Pedro River Review, Snake Nation, Southern Poetry Review, Split This Rock, Turnrow, Verse.*

The following poems appeared previously in *White Boots: New & Selected Poems of the West* (Carolina Wren Press, 2006): "At the Feast of the Last Breath" (as "Hannah's Feast"), "Wolf at the Door," "Crossing the Rez," "Upon Learning a Friend's Name May Now Be Added to the Quilt."

About the Author

William Pitt Root's work from the *New Yorker, Nation, Atlantic* and in his many collections reflect a life active both within and far away from academia, with periods working in factories, a shipyard, an underground mine, as a Teamster and as a bouncer as well as distinguished writer-in-residence positions all over the country and readings all over the world. His poetry has been translated into more than twenty languages, broadcast over Voice Of America, funded by the Guggenheim and Rockefeller Foundations, the National Endowment for the Arts, Stanford University, and the US/UK Exchange Artists program.

After the Soviet incursion into Afghanistan, of Root's long poem "The Unbroken Diamond: Nightletter to the Mujahideen," Nobel Laureate Joseph Brodsky wrote: "You are the only American poet I know of with enough heart to address this subject. And while your lines may not much help those poor people, they surely redeem this nation."

White Boots: New & Selected Poems of the West is Root's most recent collection of his own work. *Sublime Blue: Selected Early Odes of Pablo Neruda* appeared in 2013. Having taught throughout the country at Hunter College in NYC, at Amherst, Interlochen Arts Academy, NYU, Universities of Southwest Louisiana and Montana, etc. as well as on numerous reservations—and having served from 1997-2002 as Tucson's first poet laureate—Root now enjoys traveling to read, lecture, workshop and photograph around the world, including Sweden, England, Macedonia, India, Mexico, Italy, Capetown, Prague, and, recently, at the Sha'ar International Poetry Festival and at the Golden Boat Translation Conference in Slovenia. Root also serves as Poetry Editor for *Cutthroat: A Journal of the Arts*.

http://www.thedrunkenboat.com/rootview.html
http://www.cutthroatmag.com
&
http://www.coloradopoetscenter.org/poets/root_william-pitt/index.html

Colophon

The first edition of *Strange Angels* by William
Pitt Root, has been printed on 55 pound EB
"natural" paper containing a percentage of
recycled fiber. Book titles have been set in
Pablo typeface, poem titles in Georgia, and
the text in Adobe Caslon. This book was
designed by Bryce Milligan..

On-line catalogue and ordering:
www.wingspress.com
Wings Press titles are distributed to the trade by the
Independent Publishers Group
www.ipgbook.com
and in Europe by Gazelle
www.gazellebookservices.co.uk

Also available as an ebook.